A Book Of Instructions

For living with a smart modern woman in the USA

Anonymous Desert Rat

A Book of Instructions For Living With A Smart Modern Woman In the USA
Anonymous Desert Rat

Published by The Writers of the Apocalypse
1117 N Carbon Street, PMB 208
Marion, Illinois 62959
http://www.apocalypsewriters.com

For more information on Leslie Fish, visit www.lesliefish.com

Second edition
ISBN-13: 978-1-944322-10-6 Print

(License notes) ALL RIGHTS RESERVED. This book contains material protected under International and Federal Copyright Laws and Treaties. Any unauthorized reprint or use of this material is prohibited. No part of this book may be reproduced or transmitted in any form or by any means, electronic or mechanical, including photocopying, recording, or by any information storage and retrieval system without express written permission from the author / publisher.

CONTENTS

Prologue..7

Dedication...9

A Book Of Instruction For A Man Attempting To Live With The Modern Woman.............................13

Disclaimer..15

Why This Is Not An Owner's Manual....................19

It's All About Sex...21

Female Logic 25

What Kind Of Marriage Do You Want?..................31

Women Lie: That Is To Say, They Are Hardwired To Tell You What You Want To Hear..........................35

Things To Do...41

How Would You Act If She Was Your Mistress?...45

So, The Short List..47

Notes In The Book:..49

The Authors 53

PROLOGUE

Not Exactly an Owner's Manual

When I was young I thought a wife should come with an Owner's Manual, just like a new car. 50 years and 4 marriages later, I have given up on that. No modern woman with an IQ above room temperature is going to be owned. Women are a lot like cats, although more likely to come when you call them. And about as likely to do what you want when they get there as a cat. Most of us men have a fantasy of a smart wife that is a slut in the bedroom and a lady in the drawing room, and our own slave who would never look at another man. Lots of luck with that. But if you can't get a Owner's Manual, a wife should come with a book of instructions on how a man can live with her. Read this carefully and you may not have to go through 3 or 4 wives to find one you can live with.

A Book Of Instructions

DEDICATION

To my [pick one or more] Loving Husband, Live-in Boyfriend, Longtime Lover, Significant Other, Current Owner, Other_____

From your [pick one or more] New Wife, Live-in Girlfriend, Longtime Lover, Significant Other, Current Trainer, Other_____

*****

OTHER DEDICATION

This page is for the woman that was smart enough to buy this book for her man; every woman should come with a book of instructions.

If you're the man, you should start on the next page. There's nothing for you to see here. Turn the page!

Now, as I was saying, ladies, the fact that you came with a book of instructions will not get him to read it. A Real Man don't need no stinking book, ever. After all, he knows all about women. He learned it all from the bigger boys when he was young—and that's half the problem.

You see, when boys grow old enough to start getting curious about girls, who do they ask for answers? Do they ask girls, let alone women, "What do you like? How can I please you?" Oh no, never. They ask the bigger boys. And the bigger boys, for all their bragging, don't know jack-sh#t. 99.9% of them are lying virgins.

But by giving your man this book, now when you don't do what he thinks you will do, you can say: "Did you read the book? It's all there in the Instructions." Now he will have to read the book or shut up.

This book is for women with an IQ above room temperature, who can make their own way in the world, and expect to be treated as equal to their husbands. Now I know that there are a few women around who think men are superior to them, that as he worships the big GOD above, she gets to worship the little god down here—him—that her job is to be a brood mare and have a bunch of kids to fill his quiver. If you believe that, this book is not for you. Likewise if you are a Biker Mama, and your idea of a good time is when your man tells you "Strip, and get your ass up on the pool table and spread, 'cause me and my bros are horny", this book will have little to do with your lifestyle. You will find some blank pages at the end of this book where you can write down your own little dos and don'ts.

As you know, men are pretty much the same. They're kind of like Fords; you can't tell one from another. They are kind of interchangeable.

Women, on the other hand, are like hot sports cars; they have the same parts, but how you tune them makes a big difference. I have learned, the hard way, that what one woman loves another will hate. It's only fair that you list your main dos and don'ts: not all of them, just enough to give the man an idea of what he has gotten himself into. Then, when he wants to know why you're mad, just tell him it's in the book.

*****

A Book Of Instructions

A BOOK OF INSTRUCTION FOR A MAN ATTEMPTING TO LIVE WITH THE MODERN WOMAN

*This is kind of
a Coffee Table book for men
Or more like
a Bourbon Table book*

When I was young and thought it would be nice to team up with a life partner, it soon became clear to me that a woman should come with a Book of Instructions. There was nothing like that available, so I failed, and went through my first divorce. Being a slow learner, I would have more marriages and divorces. How many? Too many. It's all a blur now. And no one yet has written that Book of Instructions.

So, I am going to fulfill this need. After all, I have the experience. I have many years of trying to understand the modern woman. I have had a starter wife, a rebound wife, an I-can-do-better-than-you wife, and a trophy wife. And after a lifetime of trying to find a woman I could live with, I now have a woman I can't live without. This is because she has my meds. When I'm passed out on the floor from a heart attack, she pries my mouth open and pokes the nitroglycerin in. Or not. So far, she has kept me alive. The difference between my reason for living and the reason I'm alive is her mood. God help me if it's ever bad.

If you're like most men, the only reason you're reading this book now is that you have tried everything else and given up. You say you don't understand women. Of course not; no man does. Women do understand them, and for the most part they don't like them.

*****

DISCLAIMER

From the time I started putting pen to paper, I have had to hear my many children—and the 2 or 3 friends that I haven't yet outlived—tell me that I'm just a bitter, cynical, old man who looks back on his crappy life and failed marriages with regrets. That's not true!! I look back on my crappy life and failed marriages with no regrets; in fact, I don't consider anything a failure. Life was, and is, a learning experience. I went through a lot of pain, and am now putting it down to save you the trouble and pain I went through. See? I did it so you don't have to. It's OK. You're welcome.

Look, my background is in civil engineering, and one thing about an engineer is that he is pragmatic. He will do what works. You do not have to understand anything. Just do what works! When I tell you that flowers and chocolate will work, it has been tested. Just as I know a certain size of beam will carry a load of fixed size: it was tested. Flowers and chocolate works; it's been tested. You don't have to know why. If you try to find out why, you will go over the edge.

At this point in my life I don't have any regrets, and no hard feelings about anything. And as for the women that betrayed and deserted me, I wish them the best of all things—with whatever losers they're living with now. After all, they could have spent their last years with a prize—me—instead. So I say, bless their rotten little black hearts.

I look back on my life with all the objectivity I can come up with, in a selective-senile sort of way. I am not cynical, nor bitter; what I am is Philosophical. And that is about as good as it's going to get.

Now, I come from a family known for strong women. I'm told that I have a great-grand-aunt who got the first divorce granted in California, after it became a state—from the brother of one of the early governors. That couldn't have been easy.

In those early days, life was hard and short; people got married young and had a lot of kids, half of them died, and few people lived to reach 50, let alone beyond. The ones that lived had to be tough and know how to survive. Their outlook was fixed on living one more day. The main industries around here were mining and ranching.

There's a story about one of my great-great grandmothers, that she got married when she was, I think, 15 and he was 18. Her dad had given them a few acres, and he was working in a local mine. They had been married a week or two, and it was payday at the mine, so he stopped on the way home to have a drink or three. Then he thought it would be a good time to make sure his new bride knew who the boss was. He came home, slapped her around a bit, then lay down on the bed and passed out.

She got her needle and thread, and sewed him up in the blanket so he couldn't move. Then she got the poker from the fireplace and did her best to beat all the lumps out of that blanket. By the time her arms got tired it was getting to be light, so she went to the next farm a mile or so up the road and sent the neighbor's boy into town to get the sheriff. "Tell him I murdered my husband," she said.

Well, a few hours later the sheriff and the town doctor, who was also the coroner, came out to the ranch. They cut the husband out of the blanket, and they found out he wasn't dead. He was a little the worse for wear, but a long way from dead. Now, if this had happened today there would be no end to the trouble: jail time, divorce, court-ordered counseling, God knows what. But in those days this was looked upon as just a small bump in the road of an otherwise happy marriage. They must have made up, because they had 6 or 8 kids, 3 or 4 that lived, and their kids also had kids, down to me—who also has kids—and so it goes. They tell me that he never took another drink or hit her again. They were married 30 years or so until she died.

So now that I think about it, as I sit in my wife's little shack out here in Buttf##k, Arizona, everything in my life has been just G##D### F#####g Perfect, and I wouldn't have anything any other way. Except maybe for a new set of arteries.

See? No bitterness and not a bit cynical. Like I said, you're welcome.

*****

A Book Of Instructions

WHY THIS IS NOT AN OWNER'S MANUAL

Back in the Good Old Days (before World War One, at least), a man was the Lord of his Manor. He was the Lord and Master of the house, and woman were chattel (not *cattle,* you damn-fool Arab!). Try running that one on a modern-day woman, and she'll laugh in your face. If you're lucky.

Something went very wrong after we stopped living in caves. Back then, all you needed was a club and to be able to use it. You saw a woman you wanted to bone, and you just grabbed her and did her. (Unless, of course, she was bigger and stronger than you were—which wasn't so unlikely back in those days, when regular body-building exercise wasn't an option.) If anyone objected, you clubbed the hell out of him and had your way with her—provided she hadn't run off during all that clubbing, or grabbed a club of her own. If you liked her, you dragged her back to your cave—or maybe made her carry you—and had all of your friends come over and try out the new girl. And they would do the same for you.

In those days children were an asset, not a liability, and nobody cared about fatherhood, if they even knew about it. A child belonged to the woman that had it, and the more the better. The opinion that babies were made from woman's blood and men's sperm made sense, so the more sperm the better. None of this yours-mine-and-ours BS: just more hands to feed the tribe. A kid less than five can learn to run a trap-line, or pick fruit, or haul in a fish-trap. Now that was the good old days.

Then, sometime later on, fatherhood became recognized and everything went to hell in a handbasket. No longer could you just club your way into ownership; you had to work it out with the old owner. But you could own a woman, or as many women as you were dumb enough to want and rich enough to buy. Some men owned as many as 600. God, what that must have been like! I find just one nagging me bad enough. And imagine 600 women ganging up on you.

It's not surprising that the system changed, about the time that Lincoln freed the slaves. Women got tired of the poor quality of Lords and Masters, claimed they could do it better, got themselves property rights and the vote, and went back to body-building. No more Good Old Days.

Anyway, get any thought of ownership, or that you're the boss, out of your head if you want to live in the real world. Don't make a judge do it for you in court. No man has won Lord and Mastership in court in the last hundred years. The game is rigged, so live with it.

*****

IT'S ALL ABOUT SEX

I bet you got married for the sex—unless she has money; then you married her for the money and sex. If you only married her for the money, you will damn sure earn it.

In a marriage there are a lot of different kinds of sex, but mostly 3 kinds: #1 House Sex, #2 Bedroom Sex, and #3 Hall Sex.

When you are first together, it's house sex. That is to say, you have sex all over the house: on the kitchen counter, on the dining-room table, in the hallway standing up, on the floor in the front room, in the bathroom—and all times of the day or night: when you wake up, when you come home for lunch, when you get home from work and when you go to bed. All over, and all the time.

Then, because of all that sex, in a year or three you will have a kid or two. Kids will change your sex life. Now you only have bedroom sex, and then only at night when the kids are asleep. Not what it was, but good anyway.

After you have been together for a long time it can come down to hallway sex, and you don't want that to happen. Hallway sex is when you pass each other in the hallway and growl "F**k you" at each other. Most people divorce before then, or kill each other.

In a marriage there are a lot of highs and lows. There will be times when the sex will be as hot as when you first met. And a lot of times you just kind of take the edge off each other. But the best sex there is, is make-up sex. The only bad part of make-up sex is that you have to fight first.

There was a couple that lived across the street from me once that would have the damndest knock-down drag-out fights I ever saw. About once a month or so they would call each other names, hit each other, and break each other's stuff. This would go on till the cops would come, or sometimes it just stopped. Then, after it was quiet for a while, they would start to make up. You could hear them to the end of the block. And it went on for awhile. And boy, was it loud. If we could have got it on tape we would have had a million dollar Porno, I'm sure. I thought the fight was just foreplay, and ended as S&M sex with no safe-word.

And then there is Grudge Sex. Grudge Sex is more than just somebody had it in for you while you were away; Grudge Sex can be about getting back at anybody, anytime. Now Grudge Sex can be very good, but the only way you want it with your own wife is if she's getting even with her Ex.

There was a time, when I was between wives, that I rented a room over a bar. For awhile I thought that my purpose in life was to help wives get even with their husbands. Not a great job, but someone has to do it, and for awhile I was that Someone. Also it's risky, so make sure your front door is always patrolled by a good tough bouncer who owes you one. It helps if you're one of the bartenders.

It was then that I found out there is a female world out there that no man will ever understand. It's kind of like a different country; they speak your language, but the words don't mean the same thing. No man has ever made sense out of it. This is known as female logic. Don't even try to make sense out of it; those that do try end up in court or the funny farm, which is pretty much the same thing.

Just accept that there are things beyond your understanding, things that no man was ever meant to know. There will be many times in your marriage when your wife will say or do something that will defy logic. Do not try to make something logical out of it; just nod your head and say "Yes, dear", and go on with your happy life. Anything else will lead to a fight, a fight you cannot win, and you'll never know what it was about. A wise man (me) once said, it's better to be dumb and happy than right and logical and sleeping on the couch. If you want to get along, you'd better learn to go along.

For example, my wife is blessed with a very nice rack, and from the time she was 12 and began to bud, almost every male (she's had a few Gay friends) she's ever met couldn't wait to get her top off her, grab two big handfuls, put their head between them and make motorboat noises. Somehow she didn't find this as romantic as it sounds. When we first began to get close and I got her armor off her, I very gently lifted each breast and rubbed and scratched that area at the bottom of the bra that always itches. I worked my way around to the back, then did her back, working my way down to her feet. I spent 15 or 20 minutes rubbing her feet, worked my way back up to her shoulders, then rolled her over and told her, "Okay, you can have your way with me, now." She did! And to this day, she has her way with me whenever she wants.

The two most important words you'll ever learn are: "Yes, Dear". Stand in front of a mirror and practice them until you can say them without thinking or asking dumb questions.

*****

FEMALE LOGIC

At first this might sound like an oxymoron, but there really is such a thing. There's just no way that any man will ever understand it, so don't even try; it will only get you in trouble.

I once was friends with a particular couple; he owned a nice little company, and they had a house in the 'burbs. It was a nice place, with a pool and the works. He worked long hours and a lot of weekends. She was a stay-at-home mother of two and for the most part seemed happy, but you see, she wanted a new car. I was over at their house when they were talking about the car she wanted.

With male logic, he did not want to buy her a new car. His logic went that the car she had was only two years old, had low mileage and good tires, and ran fine, and he needed the money to make payroll and so on.

Her female logic was that if he were a Real Man, the kind she thought she had married, the kind of man that she would get her panties wet just thinking about—you know, a real smart sexy man—that such a man's wife would have the car she wanted. And anyway, her car was gray and she wanted a blue one.

And if her husband was a real man, the kind she could really love, he would see to it that she got what she wanted.

She did not say she would cut him off, but we all know the old Will She Let You, or Will She Help You, or Will She Make You Glad You Spent the Money routine.

There was a new blue car in the driveway the next time I drove by the house.

Now maybe this isn't you or me, but somewhere a man comes home from work, and all he wants is some dinner, a beer, a bit of TV, and some sleep. But he doesn't get them tonight. Tonight he gets met at the door by a very mad woman. And why is she mad? Because you are an A—hole. Now we both know that you, me, and men in general are A—holes. You were an A—hole when she met you. You were an A—hole when you were going together, and you were an A—hole when she married you. The only thing that has changed is that today you are an A—hole with a spitting-mad wife.

You might ask, "What did I do?" and she will say, "Don't pretend you don't know what you did, you A—hole! You *know* what you did, you A—hole!" Then she will storm out of the house, and there you are: no dinner, and kids that she may or may not have fed, and you don't have a clue about what you did. So you feed the kids, go buy some flowers, open a beer, put the kids to bed, watch some TV and wait.

This is female logic. All this is your fault because you are an A—hole. She, on the other hand, has gone down to a bar like the one I lived over, and found someone like me who will help her Teach You A Lesson. This is Grudge Sex at its best. There is nothing like a really mad woman putting all that energy into sex. But it isn't cheating because it was *your* fault, you A—hole. Female logic: you made her do it. She would never be there if you weren't such an A—hole.

But now, after she cleans up and starts to think, she has gotten rid of all that mad energy because she Taught You A Lesson. And, although you are an A—hole, you are *her* A—hole. And you are, after all, a nice A—hole. So now she starts to feel guilty, because although it wasn't really cheating, it kind of was. So by the time she gets home, she's in a better mood. And there you are with flowers. And you're so sorry for whatever it was you did. And now comes the best part: MAKE UP SEX! Don't think about it; just enjoy.

I have never met a man who didn't think that once in a while, outside of his marriage, some hard, noisy, sweaty, loud, no-strings-attached bit of recreational sex was kind of his due. But if his wife did it, she's a slut.

Just remember that, when you're doing it, nine times out of ten it's with someone else's wife. If you check out Craig's List you will find a lot of people looking for no-strings-attached one-night stands. It has happened that a straying husband set up a one-night stand at a bar, and when he got to the bar, waiting for him was his own wife. They've got no complaint; they were made for each other.

I remember a time, many years and 2 or 3 wives ago, when I had stopped off for a beer on the way home from work. And you know how time flies when you're drinking. I just got there, and the next thing I know they are telling me I don't have to go home, but I can't stay there; they are closing. Now in those days they had pay phones, so I went to a pay phone called home, and when a sleepy and unhappy wife answered the phone I yelled, "DON'T PAY THE RANSOM, I'VE ESCAPED!!"

It didn't work for me then, and it won't work for you now.

You remember the story of the guy complaining about being all alone. But he said that at one time he had the most wonderful wife. She was great in bed, a good cook, and kept the house spotless. She was the perfect wife. Everyone wanted to know what happened to her. Oh, she got mad at him one day, he said, and went back home to her husband.

You can never win a fight with female logic, but you can kind of use it. For instance, I am very careful when I pick a fight.

When my wife and I bought the house we live in, there was an empty lot next door. My wife wanted that lot, but the owner wanted a lot of money for it, so I talked her into waiting a year, saving up some money and making a lower offer. Sounds good, right? But as luck would have it, the owner needed to raise some money, so he put the lot on the market. Now, I knew better than to fight female logic. I hate to owe money on anything, and what I especially hate is paying interest on anything. But I went down to the bank and borrowed the money to buy the lot. See? No fight, happy wife.

We also had a long talk about how we would not spend any money we didn't have to until the loan was paid off. I did not start a fight I could not win. Now, a few days later we were buying food and I picked up some flowers and put them in the basket. My wife said "What are you doing? I thought we were not going to spend any money we didn't have to until the loan was paid off." So I put my foot down and showed her who the boss was. I said "You just spent 11K for an empty lot, and now you're going to try and tell me I can't spend a few $$ on flowers for the woman I love? I'm the boss here, and by God I will buy flowers and candy for the woman I love any time I want to."

And as I remember it, she said "Yes my lord and Master, sorry I questioned your authority. You are right." Those might not have been the exact words she used, but I'm sure that's what she meant. As you can see, I won that one.

A Book Of Instructions

WHAT KIND OF MARRIAGE DO YOU WANT?

Happy Wife, Happy Life.

My current wife is the best thing that ever happened to me. I am her first husband. She is a singer/songwriter and author. She gets, and has gotten, a lot of attractive offers from a lot of attractive people. Did she ever take up a few of those offers? You bet. I'm amazed at how few.

She wanted to marry me—in fact, she went to a lot of trouble to marry me. I would like to think she was very picky and wanted the best, so when I came along, she snagged me. For most of my life, and wives, I was just something to do 'til they got a better offer. This one got, and gets, a lot of good offers almost every day. So far, she wants to be with me. I want to keep it that way.

If you want your wife to want to be with you, make being with you a nice and happy place to be. As I said, my wife is on the road 2 or 3 times a year, gone for a week or 10 days or longer at a time. When she gets home, I meet her with flowers and a drink and draw her a bath, and I tell her how happy I am she is home and safe. She's always happy to be home with me.

There's an old story about a couple that were having trouble in their marriage. He would come home late after drinking, and she would work him over and give him what for. Someone told her to try a softer approach. So, that night when he came home after the bars had closed, when she heard him fumbling with his key trying to get it in the lock, she opened the door—dressed in her sexy see-through nightie. She pulled him in, closed the door behind him, gave him a big kiss, and said, "Let's go in the bedroom and make love." And he said, "Well, OK. I might as well. I'm going to catch hell when I get home, anyway."

Don't ever give your wife Ideas. Don't ever accuse her of things. Make your home a place you and she want to be. I know when I was in other marriages there were times when I hated to go home, because there was always some drama going on. So now I just try to make me, and this place, a person and place that she wants to be with and at. So far, it's working. It will work for you, too. Try it.

There's an old story that goes, two guys are sitting at a bar; one's trying to go home, and the other guy wants him to stay for one more round.

The first guy says, "Look, if I stay here for one more round, there will be another, and another, and the next thing I know it will be closing time, and I'll be in trouble at home, and it's just not worth it. I try everything to not have a fight. I'm as quiet as I can be. I close the garage door so I don't make any noise. I open the kitchen as quiet as I can, take off my shoes, tiptoe down the hall, even pee on the side of the bowl to not make any noise. But I open the bedroom door, and the fight is on. 'You're drunk again, you son of a bitch!' She won't let me get any sleep, and I have to go to work without any breakfast. It's not worth it, just to have a few beers."

The other guy tells him, "You're doing it all wrong. When I close this place down, I will drive very carefully—I don't want to get pulled over—'til I turn the corner on my street. Then I roar through it in first and spin the tires, fly down the street and slide into the garage, hit the table at the back of the garage, slam the garage door down, kick the kitchen door open, stomp down the hall, pee in the middle of the bowl, open the bedroom door and shout 'ANYONE IN HERE UP FOR A GOOD ROLL IN THE HAY??' …And all I hear is snoring."

This will not work for long. Don't try it.

*****

A Book Of Instructions

WOMEN LIE: THAT IS TO SAY, THEY ARE HARDWIRED TO TELL YOU WHAT YOU WANT TO HEAR

I was married to a woman for a few years that was the best actress in the world. We were both young, and she had me thinking I was the best lover that ever lived. She would have the greatest and loudest orgasms of any woman I'd ever been with. You remember the restaurant scene in the movie *When Harry Met Sally?* Well, her act was better than that.

But like all plays, sooner or later the act must end. And, with female logic, it was my fault. That's right. I wanted her to enjoy sex, so she did what I wanted her to. It was not real, but I bought it. It was my fault for not knowing my wife was lying to me. Hell, it was such a nice lie, and she ran it on me for years. But it was my fault for believing her. Now, what man is going to tell any woman, "You're lying; I'm not that good"? And by Female logic, how dare you say she's not telling the truth? You're damned if you do and damned if you don't. You can't win.

This, by the way, was the wife that left me for another woman. I have had a wife run off with a man I thought was my friend, and one run off with a woman, and one who got a better offer—or thought she could get one if I were not in the way. I made some bad picks, before I got the one I have now.

Your wife came with a book of instructions—this one—so you might want to check the pages in the back of this book marked "Things I would really like you to do". If "get a sex change" is one of them, you may want to rethink the whole marriage thing.

Women have learned a long time ago that you don't want to tell a man the truth unless it's a truth he wants to hear.

Sometimes it's not what she tells you, but what she does not tell you. Like, one of my wives told me I was the only man she ever slept with. What she did not tell me was that, with all of the other men she went to bed with, she did not sleep a wink. Not really a lie, right?

If you don't want a woman to lie to you, don't ask dumb questions.

This is a partial list of the dumb questions that every woman has been asked, and had to lie to answer. It's not a complete list nor even close, as the ignorance of men has no end. I will try to give you the lying answer you got, and the truth you don't want to hear.

#1. "Am I the best you ever had?"

For a Dumb Question like that, you deserve to be lied to. She'll answer: "Oh Baby, I never knew it could be this good. I didn't even like sex until I met you. Now I love it, but just with you."

And you believe this because it's just what you want to hear. It may even be kind of true, if you mean just today.

All the while she's thinking: "That was quick. Do I ever want to ball this A—hole again? Maybe there's hope he can learn." In other words, you just made the cut. But not by much.

Get real. Why would you think that sticking your little cigarette-size peter in her, flopping around on her belly like a fish out of water for all of about 15 seconds, screaming like a little girl, then rolling off and spending the next 10 minutes telling her how good you are would be the best she ever had? God help her if it were true. Women should have at least one good lay in a lifetime, and more than likely it's not you. So why did you ask in the first place?

The truth is, no man really cares how many men a woman has been with, as long as she'll tell him he was the best. Every man wants to think he's special.

I'll tell you what would be special: if your dick were as big as your ego. Now, that would be special. Of course, you couldn't get it into a woman if it was. Hell, you couldn't get it into your hat—not even a ten-gallon Stetson.

No woman has ever asked a man if *she* was the best *he* ever had. And why, you ask? Mostly because she couldn't care less. You got off, and that's all that matters. If you got off, it's all good. To most men a woman is just a self-lubricating masturbation device. She could be a warm melon or your hand. It's all good. What the woman is really good for is stroking your ego, more than your dick.

#2. "Did you Come?"

She'll say: "Oh yes, and it was fine, just fine."

If you have to ask, then the truth is NO. She's thinking, "Now fall asleep so I can go into the bathroom and finish what you started."

#3. "Why can't I tell when you come?"

She'll say: "I don't know. I just got carried away."

The true answer is: "Because you're never there."

When she's with the hunky pool-cleaner while you're at work, he doesn't have to ask. He has to put his hand over her mouth so the neighbors won't call the cops. In fact, after 3 or 4 good ones, she's too tired to put up with you for a day or two. Ever notice that the pool gets clean and the wife gets too tired to make love on the same day? You don't want to know why.

#4. "Is it in?"

She'll say: "Oooh, yes-yes-yes!"—or else she'll just grab it and pull it in.

If you don't know, just let her lead. If it isn't in, you don't want to know. Just enjoy, OK?

#5. "How many times did you come?"

She'll say: "So many I lost count." Right!!

She's really thinking: "What is this, a game? Do I have to keep score? What is with you men? How big, how many, how long—can't you just enjoy? Can't you just let me enjoy? Next time, bring a friend to count. Or to help. You do need help."

#6. "Was that your best time ever?"

She'll say: "O God, yes! I didn't know it could be so good."

She's thinking: "Best in the last day or two, maybe. Right now I'm trying to decide if I want to ever do you again, and ever is a long, long time. The best thing about you is how naive you are. You believe anything I tell you, so long as it's flattering."

#7. "Am I the biggest you ever had?"

She'll say: "Oh my God, yes! I thought you were

going to tear me apart. Thank you for being gentle."

She's thinking: "If it's big enough to hurt, I don't want it. Fortunately, that's not likely."

You know that a number of times, in a lifetime, she will run through that sweet tunnel a baby with a head the size of a melon, or at least a grapefruit, and her fun-thing will snap back like a rubber band, none the worse for wear. If you're going to impress a woman with size, your whanger *would* have to be as big as your ego. If it really were that big, it would take so much blood to fill it up that you'd pass out every time you got a hard-on.

#8. "Where did you learn that?"

She'll say: "I don't know, it's just you. I want to please you; I could never do that with anyone else."

You don't want to hear the truth, because it goes something like this. She's thinking: "When I was 13 or 14, the first 8 or 10 guys I gave blowjobs to, I had a hell of a time not gagging. Then I met this Black biker who was hung like a horse. After he had me, his buddies did—sometimes taking turns, sometimes 3 or 4 at a time. By the time I'd pulled this train every night or so for a few months, I learned a lot about what gets a man off. Not only that, but you could put your arm down my throat to the elbow and I wouldn't gag."

See? I told you that you didn't want to hear the truth.

*****

THINGS TO DO

So far, most of the things in this book are things you should not do. But there are a few things you should do, often. The short list is:

Flowers, Candy, Booze, and Flattery.

Let's take them in order, starting with flowers. Flowers are the best friend a man can have. From the "One perfect rose for the perfect woman", that you gave her when you first met and you were trying to get into her pants, to the armloads of them you will need after you call her by your Ex's name in bed one night. Flowers are special, and your wife is special. Show her that with flowers. Not just on birthdays, and anniversaries, and when you are an A—hole, but often. No woman ever left a man because he gave her too many flowers.

Candy: there is no such thing as too much chocolate. You could dump a truckload of chocolate on a woman, and if it crushed her to death she would die happy. And her last breath would be love for you. Unless, of course, she's allergic to chocolate. In that case, try marzipan.

Booze: this is an easy one to overdo. As you know,

the difference between the Church Lady and a biker mama is about a pint of vodka. Well, the difference between removing a few inhibitions and getting puked on is about the same amount. Taking your wife out for a drink or two once in a while, maybe even dinner, just out of the clear blue sky, is a good idea. It may only make her wonder what you have been up to, but then you can play the hurt card. You know: the "I took you out for a drink because I love you (not out of guilt over banging the guy-next-door's wife. That don't count 'cause no one found out.) This is for love." Careful you don't remove any of your own inhibitions. This is no time to confess. No one was ever divorced for something his wife didn't know.

Flattery: this is one thing that is hard to overdo, but think before you speak. Now there will be many times in a marriage when your wife will go fishing for complements. You will be going out to, say, a PTA meeting, and she will be dressing, and will say to you, "Does this dress make me look fat?" This is a loaded question. No matter how you answer it, you will be in the doghouse. If you say yes, she'll be p#ssed off for obvious reasons. If you say no, she'll think you're lying—or, worse, not even looking at her—because *she* thinks she looks fat in that dress. Whatever you do, do not say yes or no. Better you should shoot yourself. When I am asked this question I get down on the floor at her feet, put on my best puppy-dog face, and say, "Oh lovely vision of perfection, you are perfect in every way. Maybe we should not go out tonight. What if some movie star has you kidnapped and I am left to die of a broken heart? You could dress in a gunny-sack, and all the other women there in silk and satin, and you would outshine them all. You are so perfect in every way..." Lay on all of the flattery you can think of, but for god's sake don't answer that question. Just keep laying it on until she says "Okay, okay, let's go already."

It's easy to get too much booze. But too much flattery, candy, or flowers? I have never seen such a thing.

*****

A Book Of Instructions

HOW WOULD YOU ACT IF SHE WAS YOUR MISTRESS?

Remember the perfect wife that got mad and went home to her husband? Don't let that happen to you. If you treat your wife like a mistress, she might act like one. If you treat her like a wife, she might become a ex-wife. When I was young I was told by the bigger boys that a wife was a handy little gadget that you screwed on the bed, and it did the housework. Do not get in this mindset. If you act as if she was your mistress, and you wanted her to stay around, she might just stay around.

There is an old story about a woman that went to a lawyer to get a divorce. She said that her husband was the worst rat that ever lived. She hated him so much that she wanted him destroyed. She wanted to ruin him in every way she could. She wanted to make him sorry he had ever met her. She wanted to take everything they had and make all trouble for him she could. The lawyer asked if her husband hated her as much as she hated him. She said yes, that they fought almost every day. So, the lawyer told her, "If you want to really want to fix him good, don't divorce him while he hates you. Go home and pretend to love him. Do everything he wants. Make it so he can't live without you. Then when you go, boy, will that get to him. He might even kill himself." She thought about it and said, "That's a good idea. I bet I could fool him, make him think I was his little house-mouse. And then, when he was in love with me again, pull the plug. Hold the papers until I tell you." And she went home.

So a year or so went by, and the Lawyer ran into her on the street. He asked her if she was ready to file the papers yet. She said, "Oh my God, no. My husband has changed so much, I would never leave him. He is so wonderful, I don't know what got into me. I couldn't live without that man."

You cannot change another person, but you can change you—and if you do, that may change the other person too.

*****

So, The Short List

#1 Act as if your wife was your mistress.
#2 Flowers.
#3 Candy.
#4 Booze.
#4 Flattery.
#5 Read the last 2 pages of this book.
#6 When things go wrong—Just STFU.

A Book Of Instructions

NOTES IN THE BOOK:

What I Like:

_____

_____

_____

_____

What I Don't Like:

_____

_____

_____

_____

A Book Of Instructions

What I'd Really Like You To Do:

_____

_____

_____

_____

_____

What I'd Like You To Remember:

_____

_____

_____

_____

_____

Not Exactly

THE END

There's always more to learn.

A Book Of Instructions

THE AUTHORS

The Anonymous Desert Rat is really my husband, Rasty Bob Ralston—who can tell great tales but can't spell or punctuate for beans—and me, Leslie Fish—who majored in English, has worked as a newspaper editor, and published a few books. Look me up on Facebook, or catch my blog at:

http://lesliebard.blogspot.com.

I also write songs.

Find my music albums at:
www.random-factors.com

Find my books:

Offensive As Hell: The Joys of Jesus-Freak Bagging
Of Elven Blood
For Love of Glory
Revocare

WRITERS OF THE APOCALYPSE

WWW.APOCALYPSEWRITERS.COM

Publishers of Science Fiction, Fantasy, and the occasional nonfiction

THE PAGE OF CUPS: A SLIGHTLY SARCASTIC MEAD MAKER'S BOOK THAT MAY EVEN HAVE BEEN RESEARCHED SOME.

THERE'S NOTHING ROMANTIC ABOUT WASHING THE DISHES: FICTION TALES BASED ON NONFICTION EVENTS.

-OLOGIST AT LARGE: LAZY DRAWN COMICS BASED ON LIFE IN THE ARCHAEOLOGY FIELD. IT HAS JOKES.

Stop by and see us sometime
www.apocalypsewriters.com

www.ingramcontent.com/pod-product-compliance
Lightning Source LLC
Chambersburg PA
CBHW070036040426
42333CB00040B/1690